D0757563

NO LONGER PROPERTY
OF ANYTHINK
RANGEVIEW LIBRARY
DISTRICT

GOING
PRO

BECOMING A PRO
SOCCER
PLAYER

BY ANDREW PINA

Gareth Stevens
PUBLISHING

Please visit our website, www.garethstevens.com. For a free color catalog of all our high-quality books, call toll free 1-800-542-2595 or fax 1-877-542-2596.

Library of Congress Cataloging-in-Publication Data

Pina, Andrew.
 Becoming a pro soccer player / Andrew Pina.
     pages cm. — (Going pro)
 Includes index.
 ISBN 978-1-4824-2074-6 (pbk.)
 ISBN 978-1-4824-2069-2 (6 pack)
 ISBN 978-1-4824-2075-3 (library binding)
 1. Soccer—Juvenile literature. I. Title.
 GV943.25.P56 2015
 796.334'64—dc23

                                    2014033579

First Edition

Published in 2015 by
Gareth Stevens Publishing
111 East 14th Street, Suite 349
New York, NY 10003

Copyright © 2015 Gareth Stevens Publishing

Designer: Nicholas Domiano
Editor: Therese Shea

Photo credits: Cover, p. 1 peepo/Vetta/Getty Images; p. 4 Manuel Queimadelos Alonso/Stringer/Getty Images; p. 5 Hero Images/Getty Images; p. 6 Fotokostic/Shutterstock.com; p. 7 SolStock/E+/Getty Images; p. 9 Steve Bardens/Getty Images Sport/Getty Images; p. 11 Carlos Osorio/Toronto Star/Getty Images; p. 13 Steve Dykes/Getty Images Sport/Getty Images; p. 15 Shaun Botterill/Getty Images Sport/Getty Images; p. 17 Jean Catuffe/Getty Images Sport/Getty Images; p. 19 Gonzalo Arroyo Moreno/Getty Images Sport/Getty Images; p. 20 Kevin C. Cox/Getty Images Sport/Getty Images; p. 21 (background image) SasinT/Shutterstock.com; p. 21 (field) Ramcreativ/Shutterstock.com p. 22 VI-Images/Getty Images Sport/Getty Images; p. 23 Michael Steele/Getty Images Sport/Getty Images; p. 25 Francois Laplante/ FreestylePhoto/Getty Images Sport/Getty Images; p. 27 Doug Pensigner/Getty Images Sport/Getty Images; p. 29 Jamie Squire/Getty Images Sport/Getty Images.

All rights reserved. No part of this book may be reproduced in any form without permission in writing from the publisher, except by a reviewer.

Printed in the United States of America

CPSIA compliance information: Batch #CW15GS: For further information contact Gareth Stevens, New York, New York at 1-800-542-2595.

CONTENTS

Words in the glossary appear in **bold** type the first time they are used in the text.

WORLD'S MOST POPULAR GAME

Soccer is the world's most popular game. Also called association football, soccer is played in every corner of the globe, and many people play soccer for a living.

Becoming a professional soccer player takes a lot of hard work and a lot of **focus**. Game plans can be confusing, and many soccer moves are tricky, so players hoping to go pro must practice over and over. In addition, there's a lot of competition. Those who dream of going pro aren't only competing with soccer players in their own country. They're competing with millions of pro soccer hopefuls around the world.

PEOPLE OF ALL SIZES PLAY SOCCER

You don't have to be big to play soccer. World soccer star Lionel Messi—who has played for FC (Football Club) Barcelona, Spain, and the Argentinian national team—is only 5 feet 7 inches (1.7 m) tall. He was always one of the smaller players in his youth leagues, but he worked hard, practiced every day, and became one of the best players in the world.

LIONEL MESSI

In 2012, more than 3 million kids played on US Youth Soccer teams.

YOUTH SOCCER

In the United States, most soccer players start in youth leagues. There are youth leagues with players as young as 3 years old. Most kids start out in soccer at 5 or 6 years old. Most of these are **recreation** leagues.

However, talented players can join more competitive leagues. They'll be on teams with other good players and will play in tougher matches, or games. Competitive youth soccer is regional until players reach U-15 (under age 15) leagues. Then, players may compete nationally. These players may attend soccer camps run by professional coaches and might get noticed by **scouts** from soccer academies.

INDOOR SOCCER

In cold weather areas, like the northern United States and Canada, many people play indoor soccer. For young players, indoor soccer is a great way to get more playing time. The field is smaller, and the teams have fewer players. Each player gets the ball more often and can improve their shooting, passing, and ball-control skills.

Players commonly join competitive leagues around age 8. Because everyone grows at different times and learns at different speeds, players may become part of more competitive teams later on, too.

ACADEMIES

Academies are set up by professional soccer clubs, or teams, to help young players grow and improve their skills.

Promising young players are scouted from local youth leagues to join academies. Most teams in Europe have academies for players as young as 8 years old up to 16 years old. The younger players don't compete much at first. They work more on their skills, such as passing, shooting, tackling, ball control, and footwork.

At academies, players train in soccer, but also eat their meals and have tutors to help them with schoolwork. They commonly go to soccer practice after their regular school day ends.

PLAYGROUND SOCCER

Organized soccer programs aren't the only way players can improve their skills. Playground soccer offers opportunities to play against different levels of competition. Teens can play adults, and girls can play boys. Sometimes even pros will stop by! Like indoor soccer, playgrounds also often have smaller fields, so a player can get the ball more often to work on passing and dribbling.

The younger players at academies practice and play fewer hours than the teen players. Coaches want young players to learn skills without getting hurt or overworked.

By the age of 16, a player may sign a contract with the club that runs their academy. A bigger club may also purchase the player. At this point, players often begin to make a little money!

Soccer academies run by professional clubs are very common in Europe. Professional clubs in the United States don't all have academies, so sometimes players and their families travel to another state, or even another country, to train at an academy. The academy system can be tough on players, because many players are cut at each age level. Only the best players stay at the academy and become professional players.

LA MASIA DE CAN PLANES

La Masia is the academy for Barcelona, one of the biggest soccer clubs in the world. Barcelona has scouts all over the world and invites players from many other countries to join their academy. Lionel Messi was invited to try out at Barcelona. The scout flew him and his family all the way from Argentina to Spain!

English soccer player Jermain Defoe trained at Lilleshall Hall before going pro. Lilleshall Hall is a soccer boarding school on which today's academies are based.

HIGH SCHOOL AND COLLEGE

In the United States, where academies aren't as common, soccer players often play for middle school and high school soccer teams. In other countries, schools might have teams, but they're secondary to the academy teams. Upcoming American soccer star DeAndre Yedlin, for example, played for both his high school and the Seattle Sounders youth academy.

Yedlin also played college soccer at the University of Akron in Ohio. Many colleges give **scholarships** to good soccer players. At any time during a college career, a player can sign with a professional team. There are often scouts at college matches who are trying to find players that the academy system missed.

COLLEGE SOCCER

College soccer is a lot different from professional soccer. Colleges only play games in the fall, and the season has a lot of games in only a few months. They also allow unlimited **substitutions**. Professional soccer only allows three substitutions per game. However, colleges may change the rules soon to be more like the pros.

Once a college player plays on a pro team—either
overseas or in the United States—he or she can't
return to their college team. Yedlin played
2 years in college before signing with the
Sounders at age 19.

FORWARDS

How you prepare for the pros depends on your position. Each position has special skills that players need to practice to earn their place on the field.

Center forwards, or strikers, line up close to the center of the field. They're good ball handlers, so they can hold the ball after long passes. This allows their teammates to move into scoring position.

Wing forwards, or wingers, line up closer to the touchline (sideline). They're usually very fast and **agile**, so they can run by defenders. Then they pass, or cross, the ball toward the center of the field so the **attackers** can shoot the ball.

CHOOSING YOUR SPOT

What position should you play? Soccer positions are based on size, speed, and ability. Some positions require tall players to **head** the ball. Some positions need faster players to run all over the field or to keep up with other fast players. Some positions require great footwork and passing skills.

Mia Hamm was a forward who played on the US Women's National Team for 17 years. She was also part of the US women's soccer team that won Olympic gold medals in 1996 and 2004.

MIDFIELDERS

Of the 22 players on the field, midfielders have the most demanding positions to play. They have to be strong at both offense and defense.

Defensive midfielders play at the rear of the midfield. They protect the defenders from opposing attackers. They also help get the ball quickly from the defense to their own team's attackers.

Outside midfielders push the ball up the field by running along the sideline. They cross the ball to attackers and help the outside defenders.

Attacking midfielders support the forwards. They must be able to pass and shoot well. They usually have the best ball control on the team.

LONG DISTANCE RUNNING

Endurance is very important for soccer players, but especially for midfielders. In a 2014 match, US midfielder Michael Bradley ran almost 8 miles (12.9 km)! To build endurance, players not only run a lot at practice, but also run long distances during the off-season to stay in playing shape.

Midfielders need great field awareness of the players both in front of and behind them. There's so much going on around them! Xavier "Xavi" Hernández Creus of Barcelona is one of the best midfielders in the world.

DEFENDERS

Central defenders, or halfbacks, are often very tall. When the opposing team crosses the ball toward the attacking area, central defenders use their height to jump and head the ball away. They also need to be able to **tackle** well and mark (stay near) the opposing attackers during set pieces.

Outside defenders, also called fullbacks or wingbacks, need to be fast. They run along the left or right sides of the field and stay near fast midfielders and forwards. They should also be good at tackling. On offense, sometimes fullbacks run up the field to cross the ball to the attacking area.

CHANGING POSITIONS

If you start out at one position, you don't have to stay there forever. Gareth Bale, a winger for Real Madrid, started out as a fullback, but since he's really good at shooting, moved all the way up to winger. Damarcus Beasley of the Houston Dynamo has played winger, outside midfield, and left back.

A "set piece" is when the ball is returned to play after a stoppage of play, such as the ball leaving the field. Free kicks, corner kicks, and throw-ins are set pieces. Since they can often result in a goal, defenders like Real Madrid's Raphael Varane need to be in place to stop them!

KEEPERS

The goalkeeper, or "keeper," is the last line of defense. Usually, the goalkeeper is the tallest player on the team. Even though they don't have to run very fast, they need to be able to quickly react to shots. Since they're in charge of the defense, they need to know where the defenders should be, especially for free kicks.

The keeper is the only player who can use his hands. But keepers also have to be good with their feet! If the other team hits the ball over the end line, the keeper can start play again with a strong goal kick to midfield.

USA: LAND OF GOALKEEPING GREATS

Since 2001, there have been at least two goalkeepers from the United States in the English Premier League, one of the best soccer leagues in the world. The United States produces a lot of tall, athletic keepers who can keep up with the physical style of play in England. Everton's Tim Howard set the record for most saves in a World Cup match, stopping 16 shots against Belgium in 2014 in Brazil.

TIM HOWARD

PLAYER POSITIONS

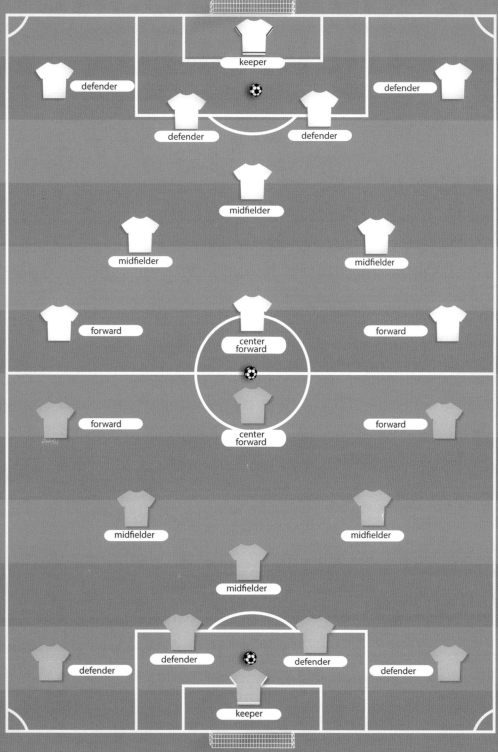

There are many ways to set up players on the soccer pitch, or field. This image shows two possible formations soccer clubs may take at the beginning of a match.

LEAGUES AROUND THE WORLD

The best leagues in the world are in Europe. These leagues have large TV contracts and are watched around the world. The biggest stars, such as Sweden's Zlatan Ibrahimovic or Portugal's Cristiano Ronaldo, are world famous.

The English Premier League (EPL) in England and Wales, La Liga in Spain, the Bundesliga in Germany, and Serie A in Italy are the top leagues. The best teams in these leagues, such as Real Madrid (La Liga) or Manchester City (EPL), buy players from smaller teams. If a player doesn't make it to one of the top leagues, there are hundreds of these smaller clubs where they can continue their career.

THE WORLD CUP

Every 4 years, countries around the world bring their best players together to play for the world championship called the World Cup. Since it began in 1930, Brazil has won five times. However, while Brazil hosted the 2014 World Cup, they lost to Germany in the quarterfinals. Germany ended up winning against Argentina in the final game with a score of 1-0.

WORLD CUP TROPHY

Many pro soccer hopefuls believe the English Premier League is the best league a player can be part of. Fans of the league are some of the most loyal and enthusiastic in all of sports, too.

MAJOR LEAGUE SOCCER

To host the World Cup in 1994, the United States had to promise to start its own league. It started Major League Soccer (MLS) in 1996. There are many players in the MLS who are older than the league! The MLS is the highest level of professional soccer in the United States and Canada. Some players reach the MLS by progressing through a team's youth academy to the senior team. Other players are **drafted** from colleges. They're also brought in from other countries.

In 2015, the MLS added two new teams in New York (NYC FC) and Orlando (Orlando City), increasing the league's size to 21 teams.

OTHER US LEAGUES

The North American Soccer League (NASL) was a pro soccer league in the United States from 1968 to 1985. It started up again in 2011 as a second-division professional league under the MLS. The United Soccer Leagues Professional Division (USL PRO) is a third-level professional league. Teams from USL PRO began **affiliations** with MLS teams in 2013 to encourage player development in the nation.

The Montreal Impact joined the MLS in 2012. It's likely that even more teams will join the league in coming years.

WOMEN'S SOCCER

Girls can be pro soccer players, too! They start out in the same way as boys, playing youth soccer, in tournaments, and eventually earning college scholarships.

The National Women's Soccer League (NWSL) is the women's professional league in the United States. The league started in 2013 with players from Canada, the United States, and Mexico.

There are many women's soccer leagues in the world. However, women's soccer isn't as big a **spectator** sport as men's soccer, making the pay a lot less. Only the very best players can make a living playing soccer. Many women must have another job, too.

TEAM USA

In the United States, very talented soccer players—girls and boys—can try out for the US Youth Soccer Olympic Development Program. If selected, they'll train with Olympic coaches, possibly for future Olympic Games, and compete with other good players from around the country. College coaches often scout players at these camps, too.

American soccer player Abby Wambach has two Olympic gold medals in soccer. She broke Mia Hamm's all-time international goal-scoring record in 2013.

INTERNATIONAL FOOTBALL

Going for the gold in the World Cup or Olympics is one of the highest goals a soccer player—man or woman—can reach. For many soccer players, this starts when they make the national team.

The full senior women's national team competes in both the World Cup and the Olympic Games. For men, it's a bit different. The senior national team competes to play in the World Cup, but the Olympic teams are mostly players 23 years old or younger. Each continent also holds a championship in which national teams may play. North America's championship is called the Gold Cup.

COPA AMÉRICA CENTENARIO

South America's soccer championship is called the Copa América. The Copa América celebrates its 100th anniversary in 2016. It's the oldest continental soccer tournament in the world. The first Copa América was held in Argentina.

From leagues to international competitions, there are many ways to play pro soccer. All it takes is talent and a lot of practice!

GLOSSARY

affiliation: having a close connection

agile: able to move quickly and easily

attacker: in soccer, a player who's trying to score

draft: to select a player from a pool of potential players entering the league

endurance: the ability to do something hard for a long time

focus: to concentrate effort or attention

head: in soccer, to hit the ball forward with the head

recreation: something you do for fun or as a hobby

scholarship: money awarded to a student to pay for education

scout: the person who searches for people with great skills in a sport. Also, to conduct the search.

spectator: someone who watches an event

substitution: an exchange of players during a sports game

tackle: in soccer, the act of meeting an opponent and taking the ball away using the feet

FOR MORE INFORMATION

Books

Haw, Jennie. *Score! The Story of Soccer*. New York, NY: Crabtree Publishing Company, 2014.

Robertson, Kay. *Soccer*. Vero Beach, FL: Rouke Educational Media, 2013.

Sosa, Carlos. *Lionel Messi*. Broomall, PA: Mason Crest, 2013.

Websites

Laws of the Game
www.ussoccer.com/referees/laws-of-the-game
Review the rules of professional soccer.

The Official Website of the World Cup
www.fifa.com/worldcup/
Read more about the most recent World Cup, players, and the future of the game.

Publisher's note to educators and parents: Our editors have carefully reviewed these websites to ensure that they are suitable for students. Many websites change frequently, however, and we cannot guarantee that a site's future contents will continue to meet our high standards of quality and educational value. Be advised that students should be closely supervised whenever they access the Internet.

INDEX